# Do You Take Turns?

3 1389 01984 2574

## by Joanne Mattern

**Reading consultant:** Susan Nations, M.Ed., author/
literacy coach/consultant in literacy development

**WEEKLY READER®**
PUBLISHING

**Please visit our web site at: www.garethstevens.com**
**For a free color catalog describing our list of high-quality books,**
**call 1-800-542-2595 (USA) or 1-800-387-3178 (Canada).**

Library of Congress Cataloging-in-Publication Data

Mattern, Joanne.
    Do you take turns? / Joanne Mattern.
       p. cm. — (Are you a good friend?)
    Includes bibliographical references and index.
    ISBN-10: 0-8368-8276-8 (lib. bdg.)
    ISBN-13: 978-0-8368-8276-6 (lib. bdg.)
    ISBN-10: 0-8368-8281-4 (softcover)
    ISBN-13: 978-0-8368-8281-0 (softcover)
    1. Sharing in children—Juvenile literature.  2. Friendship
in children—Juvenile literature.  I. Title.
BF723.S428M38   2008
177'.62—dc22               2007011024

First published in 2008 by
**Weekly Reader® Books**
An imprint of Gareth Stevens Publishing
1 Reader's Digest Road
Pleasantville, NY 10570-7000 USA

Copyright © 2008 by Gareth Stevens, Inc.

Editor: Gini Holland
Art direction: Tammy West
Graphic designer: Dave Kowalski
Picture research: Diane Laska-Swanke
Photographer: Gregg Andersen
Production: Jessica Yanke

Printed in the United States of America

1 2 3 4 5 6 7 8 9 11 10 09 08 07

# Note to Educators and Parents

Reading is such an exciting adventure for young children! They are beginning to integrate their oral language skills with written language. To encourage children along the path to early literacy, books must be colorful, engaging, and interesting; they should invite the young reader to explore both the print and the pictures.

The *Are You a Good Friend?* series is designed to help children learn the special social skills they need to make and keep friends in their homes, schools, and communities. The books in this series teach the social skills of listening, sharing, helping others, and taking turns, showing readers how and why these skills help establish and maintain good friendships.

Each book is specially designed to support the young reader in the reading process. The familiar topics are appealing to young children and invite them to read — and reread — again and again. The full-color photographs and enhanced text further support the student during the reading process.

In addition to serving as wonderful picture books in schools, libraries, homes, and other places where children learn to love reading, these books are specifically intended to be read within an instructional guided reading group. This small group setting allows beginning readers to work with a fluent adult model as they make meaning from the text. After children develop fluency with the text and content, the books can be read independently. Children and adults alike will find these books supportive, engaging, and fun!

— Susan Nations, M.Ed., author, literacy coach,
and consultant in literacy development

Are you a good friend?
One way to be a good
friend is to take **turns**.
Do you know how to
take turns?

Taking turns means everyone has a chance to play. There are many ways to take turns.

You can take turns on the playground. Taking turns helps make playtime safe.

You can take turns at school. Taking turns gives everyone a chance.

You can take turns at home. It is easy to **wait** your turn when you are having fun.

Sometimes, taking turns is hard. Sometimes, you want your turn right away!

15

Taking turns is **fair** to everyone. When you take turns with others, you can all get what you need.

Taking turns often means waiting. It is easy to wait when you know your turn is coming.

Taking turns is an important way to be a good friend!

# Glossary

**fair** — treating everyone the same

**turns** — chances to do or get something

**wait** — to do nothing until it is your turn

# For More Information

*It's My Turn!* Heather Maisner (Kingfisher)

*Now It's Your Turn.* You and Me (series). Denise M. Jordan (Heinemann Library)

*Share and Take Turns.* Learning to Get Along (series). Cheri J. Meiners (Free Spirit Publishing)

*Taking Turns.* Janine Amos (Cherrytree Books)

# Index

## About the Author

**Joanne Mattern** has written more than 150 books for children. Joanne also works in her local library. She lives in New York State with her husband, three daughters, and assorted pets. She enjoys animals, music, reading, going to baseball games, and visiting schools to talk about her books.

391.009   Ruby, Jennifer.
R            The 1980s / Jennifer Ruby. -- London :
         Batsford, c1990.

             64 p. : ill. -- (Costume in context)

             ISBN 0-7134-6539-5: $19.95

                             14542

                             FEB      1992

             1. Costume--Great Britain--History--20th
         century.    I. Title.   II. Series.

# Costume in Context
# The 1980s

*Jennifer Ruby*

B.T. Batsford Ltd, London

# Foreword

When studying costume it is important to understand the difference between fashion and costume. Fashion tends to predict the future – that is, what people *will* be wearing – and very fashionable clothes are usually worn only by people wealthy enough to afford them. For example, even today, the clothes that appear in fashionable magazines are not the same as those being worn by the majority of people in the street. Costume, on the other hand, represents what people are actually wearing at a given time, which may be quite different from what is termed 'fashionable' for their day.

Each book in this series is built round a fictitious family. By following the various members, sometimes over several generations – and the people with whom they come into contact – you will be able to see the major fashion developments of the period and compare the clothing and lifestyles of people from all walks of life. You will meet servants, soldiers, street-sellers and beggars as well as the very wealthy, and you will see how their different clothing reflects their particular occupations and circumstances.

Major social changes are mentioned in each period and you will see how clothing is adapted as people's needs and attitudes change. The date list will help you to understand more fully how historical events affect the clothes that people wear.

Many of the drawings in these books have been taken from contemporary paintings. During the course of your work perhaps you could visit some museums and art galleries yourself in order to learn more about the costumes of the period you are studying from the artists who painted at that time.

# Acknowledgments

I would like to acknowledge the sources for the following: Pages 26 and 27, after fashion designs by John Ireland. Colour plate 'Fashion 1985' after fashion drawings by Isao Yajima.

I would also like to thank Liz Wright for her help with page 58.

© Jennifer Ruby 1990
First published 1990

Typeset by Tek-Art Ltd, Kent
and printed and bound in Great Britain
by The Bath Press, Avon
for the publishers
B.T. Batsford Ltd
4 Fitzhardinge Street
London W1H 0AH

ISBN 0 7134 6539 5

# Contents

# Date List

**1979** Mrs Thatcher became the first woman Prime Minister in Britain. Punk styles were still popular with many young people.

**1980** The clothers store Dash is formed, mixing sport with fashion.

**1981** Vivienne Westwood launched her 'Pirates and Romantics' look which was popularized by Adam and the Ants.
Prince Charles and Lady Diana Spencer were married at St Paul's Cathedral.
Culture Club hit the charts, and there was a brief vogue for cross-dressing inspired by Boy George.

**1982** The Next stores were launched, introducing smart, stylish clothers at affordable prices.
Videos become an essential part of pop singles, as the influence of the American channel MTV, showing videos exclusively, spread to Britain.

**1983** Madonna's first album, *Like a Virgin*, was released.
The word 'Yuppie' came into use to describe young, upwardly-mobile executives characterized by slick city clothes, Porsches and portable phones.

**1984** Band Aid was formed and made 'Do they know it's Christmas?' to raise money for Ethiopia. Bob Geldof, the organizer, inspired the trend for a scruffy, unkempt image.

**1985** 13 July: Live Aid Concert carried on the Pop Industry's work for charity.
*EastEnders* started.

**1986** The return of the mini.
Fifties revival, seen in films such as *Absolute Beginners* starring David Bowie.

**1989** The Green Party achieved unexpected success in the European elections as the environment became a national concern.
The corset company Spirella closed – women had at last achieved liberation!

# Introduction

Fashion always mirrors the age in which it lives, and the fashions of the 1980s were no exception. Clothes became more varied than ever before, and it was difficult to identify any one particular style as being the current 'fashion'. However the many different images to be seen both in the street and on the catwalk were merely reflecting the nature of society in the 1980s.

Britain had a woman Prime Minister for the duration of the decade, and many other women started up successful businesses or pursued high-powered careers; for example, Anita Roddick's The Body Shop, with its natural cosmetics and direct opposition of experiments on animals, became a thriving international company, with over 200 shops all over Britain. Women's clothes moved closer to men's in the world of business, with a style known as 'Power Dressing': smart suits, exaggerated shoulder lines and shoulder pads, shirts and neckties, and short, sleek hairstyles. The enterprise culture had arrived, and money now equalled success, facts which affected men's clothes too. The suit gained in significance and became a standard item for anyone competing in the tough business world. Ties also changed from being a necessary and dull accessory to a colourful and fun addition to a man's wardrobe.

In direct contrast to this were the fashions known as 'street style'. These were clothes that were outside Establishment approval and were designed to challenge and shock. The designer Vivienne Westwood commented that 'street style had a content', in other words it was usually a statement or expression of something and was therefore outside the accepted mode of dressing. The aggressive Punk styles that originated in the late 1970s were a good example of this. They were subversive and anarchic and represented the anger of a generation of young people who keenly felt the realities of unemployment.

Ironically, the originality of the 'anti-Establishment' clothes of street style meant that they were often taken up by designers who turned them into high fashion, thus making them acceptable to the majority.

The 1980s also saw increased concern over environmental and social issues, and this was also reflected in fashion. Katherine Hamnett, for example, popularized the T-shirt-with-a-slogan idea with her '58% don't want Pershing' shirt, which she wore to 10 Downing Street, and Bob Geldof presented a scruffy, unkempt image for his Live Aid work which seemed to be making a deliberate statement that appearance and grooming are unimportant when it comes to saving the world.

The media continued to have a direct influence on fashion with TV, films, art and pop music all playing an important part. Soap operas were popular and presented an array of different styles from the decorative and extravagant glamour of Joan Collins' power dressing in *Dynasty* to the working class fashions of *EastEnders*. Pop stars like

Madonna with her provocative appearance, George Michael with his 'designer stubble' and Annie Lennox with her cropped hair and men's suits presented images that were imitated by thousands of young people. Another important influence portrayed through mass media was the elegant and groomed style of the Princess of Wales, whose hairstyle and clothes were copied by women throughout the world.

The many different nationalities who migrated to Britain during the 1960s and early 1970s brought their own fashions with them, many of which had been integrated into the mainstream by the 1980s. In addition, top designers frequently gave their collections an ethnic theme, with shapes, patterns and colour mixes based on the traditional designs of different national costumes.

The health and fitness boom that originated in the 1970s continued throughout the 1980s, creating a demand for fashionable exercise clothes. Colourful track suits, ski-pants, sweatshirts and shorts were seen as much in the streets as on the sports field. Once again, sporting clothes became fashion garments.

The 1980s therefore saw a confusion of different styles without the strong emergence of anything new. There was much nostalgia for the past with the revival of many old styles, for example, a vogue for antique lace, thirties knitwear, rock 'n' roll skirts and the mini. When fashion looks to the past for inspiration, it is sometimes a sign that all is not well in society, and in the economically gloomy climate of the early 1980s many found it more fun to escape into the past than to face up to reality. What *was* new about the decade was the freedom of expression. People could at last choose to wear whatever they wished without being tyrannised by the dictates of fashion.

# A Company Director, c. 1980

This is John Barnes who is one of the directors of a large oil company. Much of his time is spent at the company's head offices in London, and when he is there John is always immaculately dressed. In the picture he is wearing a dark navy pin-stripe suit, a white cotton shirt and a dark tie with a matching handkerchief in his breast pocket.

John is wealthy and can afford expensive, quality clothes. Other items from his wardrobe are pictured opposite and include a Burberry coat. This is a light, good-quality raincoat, the material for which was originally designed by Thomas Burberry of Hampshire in the nineteenth century. He called the material 'gaberdine', and it was so successful that Burberry weather-proofs were worn by officers in the Boer War and a coat of this material specifically designed for trench warfare appeared in 1914. The trench coat as we know it today still retains the authentic details, for example, the storm flap on one shoulder, the epaulettes and D-rings on the belt (used to clip on military equipment).

John's wardrobe also includes many shirts, jumpers and trousers and numerous outfits for the various sports he enjoys.

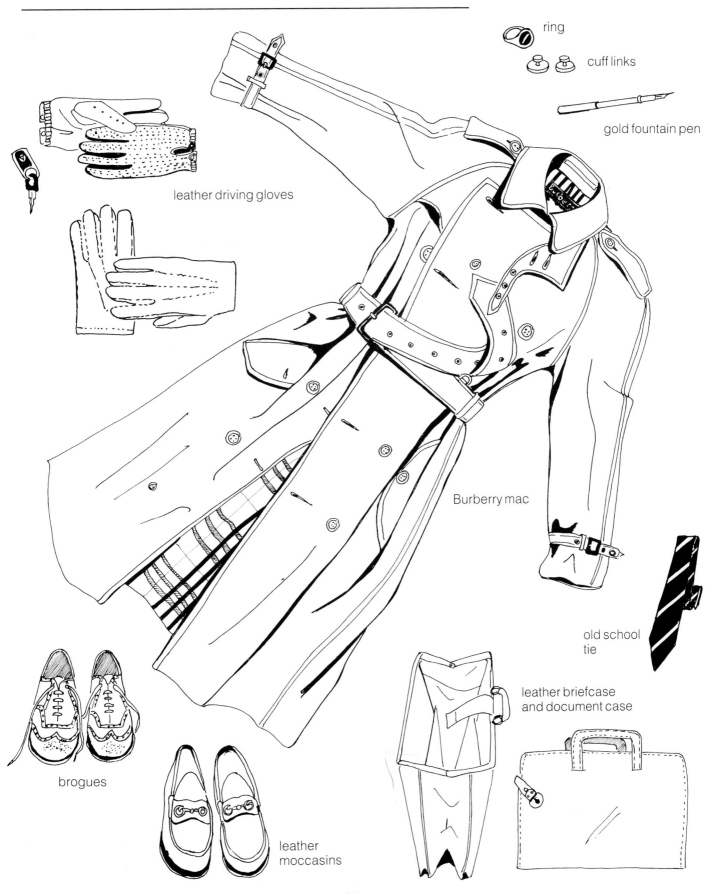

ring

cuff links

gold fountain pen

leather driving gloves

Burberry mac

old school
tie

leather briefcase
and document case

brogues

leather
moccasins

# The Owner of a Beauty Salon, c. 1980

This is John's wife, Marcia, who owns a hairdressing and beauty salon. As she is so busy managing her home and business, Marcia prefers elegant, classic styles that are comfortable and easy to wear. In this picture she is wearing a loose-fitting linen dress and jacket in white and beige which is smart without being too formal. Her hair is worn at shoulder length and has been lightly permed for her by one of her staff.

Other items from her wardrobe are pictured on the opposite page.

Marcia is typical of many women of the 1980s who successfully managed to combine their careers with family life. These women created a demand for smart, stylish clothes and projected an image of efficiency and elegance, showing that concern about appearance could go hand in hand with success in the tough world of business.

Indeed, perhaps following the leader Margaret Thatcher (who, it is said, took her heated rollers with her on her postwar visit to the Falkland Islands) and successful businesswomen of the 1980s, women now proved that they could be efficient, successful and even ruthless, but also attractive.

fitted pink suit
with black trim

neckties

red leather
glove with
gold bracelet

co-ordinating
two-piece in
cotton

blouson
jacket

calf-length
tweed skirt

# Children's Clothes, c. 1980–1985

Here is 13-year-old Christopher, John and Marcia's son, who attends one of the local schools. He loves to talk to his father about the oil rigs and plans to make a career in the oil industry when he grows up. Christopher likes practical, rugged clothes and in the picture he is wearing a polyester and cotton mix jacket over a checked cotton shirt and denim jeans.

During the 1980s, clothes manufacturers began catering more for the younger teenage market. Some chain stores created special 'teen' fashions aimed at the 9–14 age range as young girls were becoming increasingly fashion conscious. The styles tended to follow women's fashions and included smart and casual wear. You can see one of Christopher's friends wearing an example of one of these styles on the opposite page.

Clothes for younger children continued to be colourful, practical and hard wearing. T-shirts, jeans and corduroys were popular and came in a vast range of colours. Chains like Dash and Benetton set up special children's departments carrying a range of children's casual styles that were miniature replicas of their adult range. Three of the children from Christopher's neighbourhood are pictured opposite wearing their favourite outfits.

cotton blouse,
denim dungarees,
canvas shoes

sweatshirt
jeans

cotton T-shirt
wool skirt
cotton socks
leather sandals

In previous centuries, wealthy children were often dressed as miniature adults and suffered the same corsets, tight-lacing, starched frills and ruffles as their parents. In the 'liberated' 1980s fashion was being aimed at younger and younger children and it is interesting to speculate whether four-year-olds dressed in fashions that mirrored their parents' were as uncomfortable as their ancestors!

teen fashion:
print cotton
skirt and
matching top

# Pirates and Romantics, c. 1981

Following on the heels of the anarchic punk styles of the late 1970s and early 1980s was a brief period of fantasy dressing. Like punk, the look was launched by the designer Vivienne Westwood and her partner Malcolm McClaren and was popularised by the pop groups Adam and the Ants (see page 28) and Bow Wow Wow. The new looks were called 'Pirate' and 'New Romantic' and started a vogue for frilly-fronted shirts, waistcoats and layers of patterns and different textures.

This is Adrienne, Christopher's sister who is at art college. She is dressed in the pirate style and has created her swashbuckling, buccaneer appearance with a bold use of pattern and layers. Her checked coat has been slashed at the inner sleeves of both arms to reveal the overall beneath. This is a straight, smock-like affair which is worn over a long shirt with frills at the cuffs. She has tied a spotted, tassled band around her waist, and her hair is tied back in pirate fashion. Her patterned stockings are held up with garters and she is wearing suède boots. The look is completed with a theatrical hat and large hoop earrings.

Adrienne's friend Jennifer prefers a softer, more romantic look. She is wearing a cotton blouse with a ruffled front, a dark cotton skirt with a wide waist held in with a belt and a white cotton petticoat. Her hair is deliberately tangled.

Vivienne Westwood was a very important designer in the 1980s. After the excitement of the swinging sixties when London had led the fashion world, the 1970s had been a barren time when Britain was virtually ignored as a fashion centre, with designers seemingly lacking in direction. Westwood single-handedly diverted attention back to Britain by overturning preconceived ideas of what clothing should be about. Her Punk, Pirate and later, Hobo and Savage collections were innovative, exciting and challenging. Although initially her ideas were laughed at, eventually they were appropriated by other designers and appeared at the top end of the market.

# On an Oil Rig, c. 1981

Sometimes John Barnes visits some of the oil rigs owned by his company and he usually takes a couple of engineers with him from Head Office to check how things are going.

This is Karen, a petroleum engineer. She is highly qualified and is going to check the well log, which is a systematic recording of data about the well which has to be analysed. The rig is offshore and Karen and the others had to fly out to it by helicopter. She is wearing a protective overall made from heavy cotton, a hard hat, safety boots and gloves. The hard hat and safety boots are compulsory wear for anyone on the rig. The boots have steel caps in the toes which help to protect them if a heavy weight were dropped onto them. They also have steel shanks in the soles in case the wearer were to step onto a sharp object.

Working clothes like dungarees and Dr Marten shoes made their way onto the streets during the 1980s as both men and women reacted against 'designer dressing' (see page 34).

On the right you can see some Roughnecks who are putting a drill pipe down the well hole. This process is called 'tripping in'. Roughneck is the name used for a worker on a drill rig. It is hard, heavy work and the men often get covered in mud. All three are wearing hard hats, safety boots and gloves and the two men on the right also have on protective overalls. In the winter time they sometimes wear quilted overalls as these are much warmer.

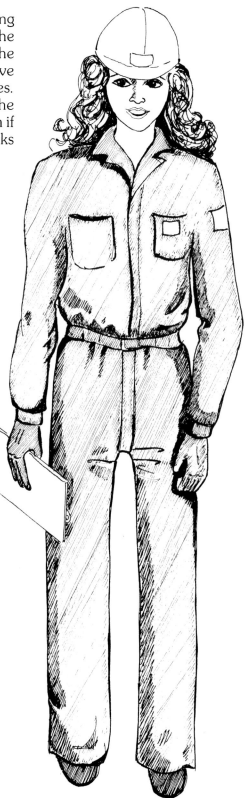

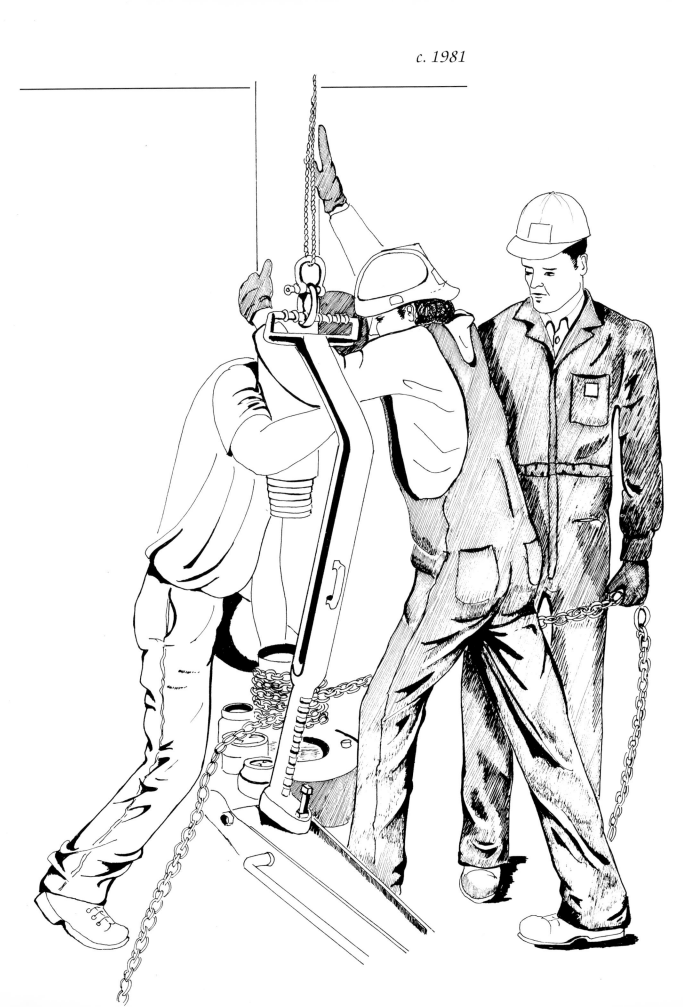

# A Royal Wedding, c. 1981

On 29 July 1981, the wedding of Prince Charles and Lady Diana Spencer was like a fairytale at a time of high unemployment and depression. When Diana stepped from her coach in a froth of ivory silk the whole world seemed to stop to look.

Designed by David and Elizabeth Emanuel, the dress was unashamedly romantic, made of pure ivory silk taffeta and old lace and hand embroidered with 10,000 pearls and mother-of-pearl sequins. The neckline and sleeves were trimmed with lace flounces, and the sweeping train, 25 feet long and detachable, was trimmed and edged with sparkling lace.

coatdress with
sailor collar
and matching
tricorn hat

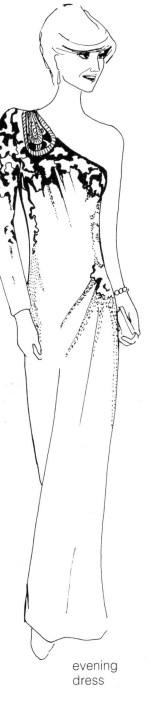

evening
dress

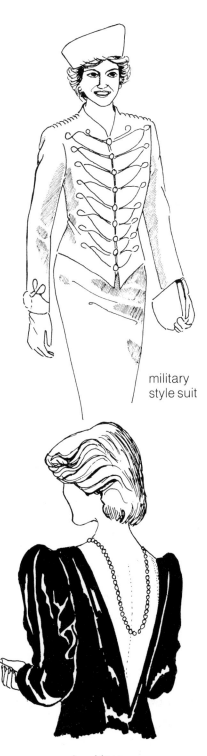

military
style suit

backless
evening dress
with pearls worn
down back

The Princess of Wales became an important fashion leader in the 1980s, supporting British fashion designers such as Bruce Oldfield and Arabella Pollen. Her daytime clothes, usually classic, tailored dresses and suits, were popular with the 30-45 age group and imitated by shops such as Alexon and Jaeger. Her evening clothes were more glamorous, with off-the-shoulder ballgowns and slim, sequinned dresses, and were taken up by women of all ages. Diana also did much to revive a flagging millinery trade, with her many hats that thousands of women sought to copy.

You can see some of the more striking outfits that she wore during the 1980s on this page and also in the colour section of the book.

19

# The Country Look, c. 1983

John and Marcia Barnes own a cottage in the country. They often spend their weekends there and find it restful and peaceful after the stresses of work.

The clothes they wear in the country reflect the more relaxed lifestyle that they adopt there.

In this picture John is wearing a green corduroy suit composed of a double breasted jacket, a waistcoat and matching trousers. He also has on a woollen checked shirt, a plain wool tie and a scarf around his neck.

Marcia is wearing a Barbour, which is a waxed cotton jacket. John Barbour went into business in 1890, producing waterproof jackets. The design remained very popular and the Barbour has now become the classic country jacket. The waxed cotton is tough and waterproof and the olive colour is perfect country camouflage! The coat has a tartan body liner and a corduroy-faced collar.

Marcia is also wearing a woollen sweater and a herringbone cap and skirt.

Marcia and John like to go for long country walks. When they do they wear almost identical outfits – Barbour coats, peaked caps, sweaters, corduroy trousers and walking shoes or Wellington boots. They also add gloves and scarves if the weather is cold.

woollen gloves

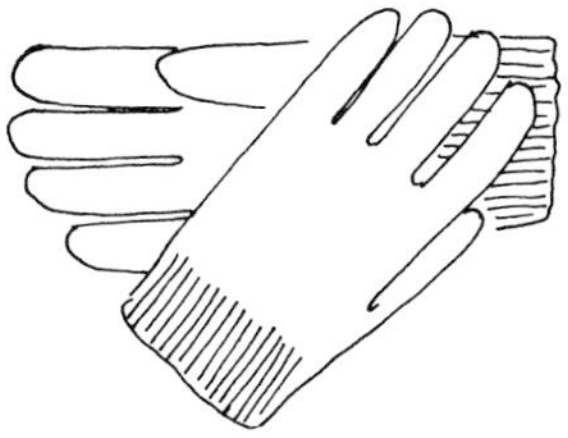

walking/casual shoes

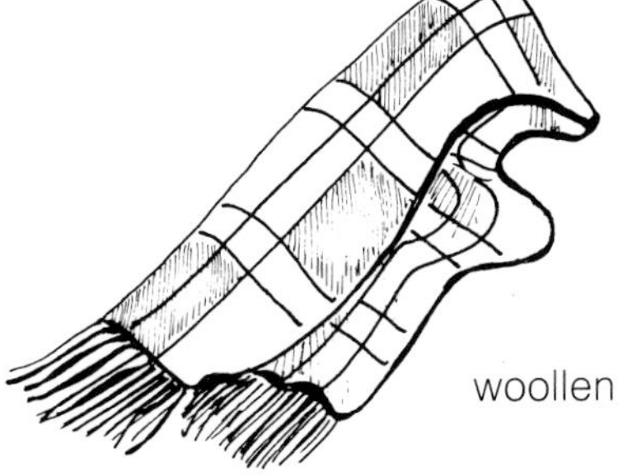

woollen scarf

wellington boots

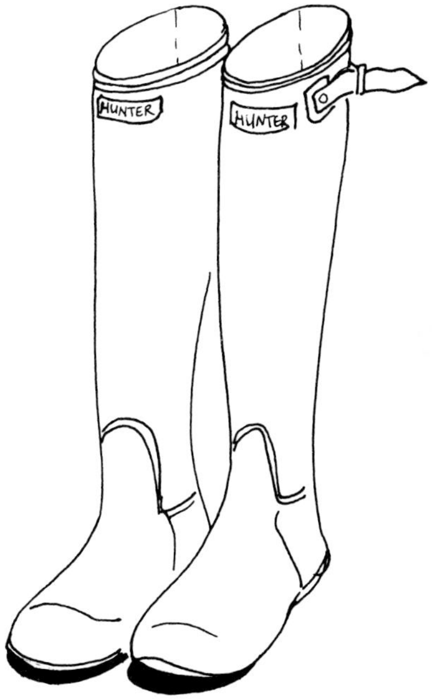

21

# A Country Visit, c. 1983

Adrienne likes to stay at her parents' cottage and often goes there during the college holidays with some of her friends.

On the right she is wearing sensible country clothes and is ready for a long walk. Her outfit consists of a trilby hat, a warm woollen jumper and matching cardigan, a wool skirt, a herringbone coat, thick socks and gloves and brogues.

Adrienne still likes to dress in an individual way and often purchases her clothes from second-hand and antique shops and markets. On the opposite page she is wearing an antique lace blouse, cotton bloomers and a hand-knitted bobble sweater. She also enjoys collecting ethnic clothes and jewellery. On her feet she is wearing soft leather moccasins and she has a Mexican rug around her shoulders.

*c. 1983*

When in the country, Adrienne likes to try out some traditional country crafts. On the wall behind her you can see two hats which she decorated with dried flowers, two hand-printed cotton aprons and a cloth bag which she made herself.

# A Hairdresser, 1984

This is Marcia's niece Gabrielle who works for Marcia in the hairdressing and beauty salon. Gabrielle likes to keep up with the latest fashions although she has to be content to wear an overall while at work. In this picture she is wearing a military-look suit in white linen with a black leather belt. Her hair has been 'crimped' with special tongs to give it the crinkly effect that is currently fashionable.

In her work Gabrielle needs to be skilled at creating many different hairstyles to suit the needs of her customers. Some of these styles are influenced by the many ethnic groups in Britain. A good example of this can be seen on the opposite page where a white woman's hair has been woven close to the head in a manner similar to the two traditional African styles shown above. The 'Afro' perm and 'scrunch' drying, (tangling and crumpling the hair when wet), are two more popular hairstyling techniques which give a thicker, more curly look.

At the other end of the scale, Gabrielle is often asked to create short, sporty styles suited to the hectic lifestyle of the 1980s woman. Sometimes the customer asks for brightly coloured streaks and a 'spiky' effect. This, of course, is a legacy from Punk. Can you think of any more unusual hairstyles from the 1980s?

traditional
African hair-styles

hair plaited close to the head
in four spirals

hair closely woven
on one side of the
head (like knitting)

hair permed then
'scrunched' dry

hair shorter and
darker underneath

a short crop with
coloured streaks

# Casual and Sporty, c. 1984

When she is not working, Gabrielle enjoys dressing in the latest fashions. On this page she is wearing a velvet cap, a knitted sleeveless top, a silk blouse, a checked woollen skirt with large pockets, a wide leather belt and ankle boots.

On the opposite page you can see other items from her wardrobe. She particularly likes wearing her 'ra-ra' skirt when she goes to parties or discos as it is light and easy to dance in. The 'ra-ra' skirt is characterised by its flounces and is reminiscent of the styles worn by Spanish flamenco dancers.

Gabrielle often listens to pop music. Over the next few pages you can see some of her favourite stars.

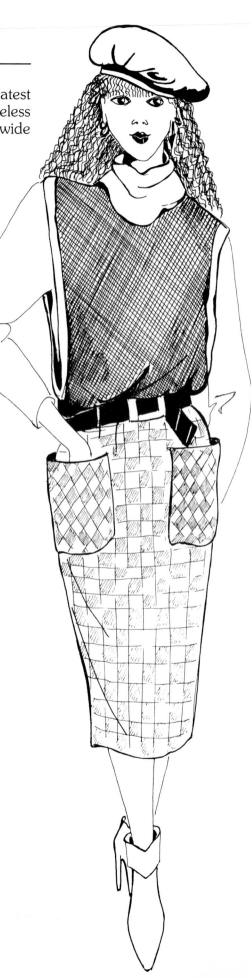

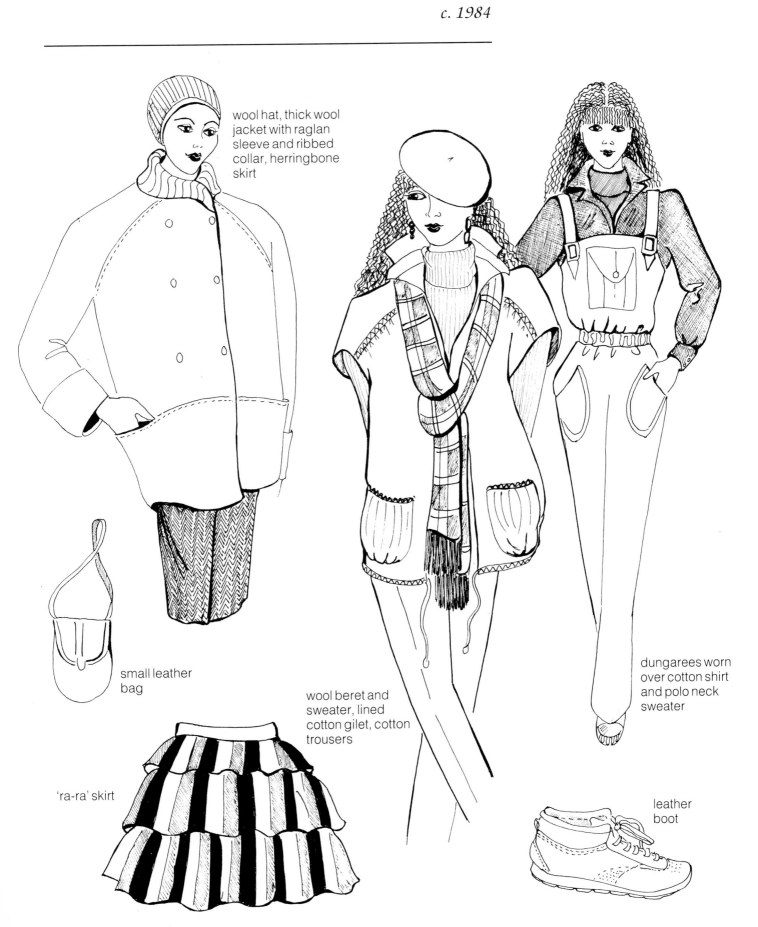

wool hat, thick wool jacket with raglan sleeve and ribbed collar, herringbone skirt

small leather bag

'ra-ra' skirt

wool beret and sweater, lined cotton gilet, cotton trousers

dungarees worn over cotton shirt and polo neck sweater

leather boot

# The Influence of Pop Music in the 1980s

During the 1980s an enormous influence was exerted by pop music on the world of fashion. Until World War II art and fashion had been closely linked with designers reflecting the thinking of painters and sculptors. By the end of the 1950s and early 1960s however, popular music had replaced art as a major fashion influence with stars like the Beatles, Jimi Hendrix and the Rolling Stones setting new trends in music and clothes that were copied by thousands of young people.

What had felt extreme in the 1960s however seemed quite tame 20 years on as more and more bizarre styles came and went while the young experimented with sounds and images. Over the next few pages you can see just some of the image makers and breakers of the decade who inspired thousands to copy their looks.

Adam Ant in his 'pirate' gear
c. 1981

Annie Lennox, close cropped
hair and suits

Boy George, hair extensions
and make-up
c. 1982

Adam Ant (left) with his 'pirate' gear and American Indian warpaint
presented a swashbuckling image that he claimed was designed to
bring colour, showmanship and romanticism back into pop, while
Annie Lennox of the Eurythmics and Boy George from Culture Club
confused sexual boundaries with their dressing. Lennox wore her hair
cropped short and was seen in 'men's' attire while Boy George dressed
in frocks, wore make-up and talked frequently about his bisexuality.

# More Image Makers . . . c. 1985

Madonna was educated in a Catholic school and liked the crucifixes worn by the nuns. She later took to wearing them herself along with bra tops and a bare midriff, thus combining religious and sexual imagery. Once, when unable to find anything to tie her hair back with, she used an old pair of tights and immediately started another fashion trend, though most imitators used scarves instead of their discarded tights.

George Michael (from Wham) was another popular figure who portrayed a very masculine look with his leather jacket, jeans and designer stubble, while Prince, pictured opposite in a shirt with a ruffled front, velvet jacket and make-up, presented a dandy image reminiscent of the days of Beau Brummell.

Some of these images were initially designed to be deliberately shocking or bizarre yet as they were copied by thousands of young people they became more familiar and therefore more acceptable.

Can you think of any other pop stars who have had an influence on fashion?

Madonna, pearls, crucifixes, lace gloves and bra, net skirt c. 1984

George Michael – leather jacket, jeans, close-cropped beard c. 1985

Prince – velvet jacket, silk shirt with ruffled front, silk head band, make-up c. 1985

# Street Performers, c. 1985

Here are two more performers with their own individual music and style. U Roy and his girlfriend are street performers and earn quite a good living playing their guitars and singing in the streets of London.

U Roy is a Rastafarian and wears his hair in dreadlocks. He is wearing a cotton print shirt over a T-shirt, jeans and sunglasses. His girlfriend Jo is wearing a sleeveless T-shirt with a straight skirt and she has tied a bright scarf around her head.

*The Princess of Wales*

1984 – Maternity Suit

1982 –
Colourful tweed coat

1985 – velvet gown with lace insets

some of the famous hats

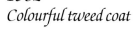

1985 – red silk crêpe

*Designer fashion*
*Left: Soprani, 1982*
*Right: Yves Saint Laurent, 1980*

*Designer Fashion:*
*Left, Lacroix, 1988*
*Right, Westwood, 1983*

*Children's Clothes, c. 1985*

*Leisure Wear, c. 1987*

*Young Fashion, c. 1988*

*Fashion, c. 1985*

# Street Style, c. 1985

One of the most interesting phenomena of 1980s fashion was the influence of 'street style'. Street fashions originated with young people and were 'anti-style' because the traditional rules of taste and fashion were deliberately broken in order to produce clothes of great originality and, sometimes, great vulgarity. The punk styles of the late 1970s and early 1980s were a good example of this, (see page 64), as they were outside Establishment approval and deliberately designed to challenge and shock.

Ironically, the originality of these 'anti-style' clothes meant that they were often copied by designers who then turned them into high fashion. There was therefore a reversal of the usual fashion influence from the top to the bottom of society – instead, fashion travelled from the bottom to the top.

Here is Jennifer, whom you last saw on page 15. She has now left Art college and is working as a graphic designer in London. She likes to dress in her own idiosyncratic style and cares little for current 'fashion'. She is wearing a black and white patterned top over a tight black jersey dress. Underneath this she has on a black and white skirt. Her hair has been cut short, dyed black and soaped in order to make it stand up. Unusual earrings, thick socks and heavy shoes complete her outfit.

# Street Chic, c. 1985

Here are three of Jennifer's friends, all of whom like to create their own individual style in dress. Alma (this page), is wearing a velvet cap, a heavy cotton coat with corduroy trim, baggy dungarees, socks and heavy leather boots like the work clothes on page 16.

On the opposite page you can see Samantha and Kate. Samantha is wearing a black velvet hat and T-shirt, a black and white jacket which she designed and made herself, checked baggy shorts, tight black leggings, socks and slip-on shoes. Her eye make-up and lipstick are black and contrast sharply with her white powdered face.

Kate has cut her hair very short and is wearing a heavy woollen jacket with satin cuffs, a black and white floral shirt, white baggy trousers and leather boots.

It is interesting that all three outfits do nothing to emphasize the female figure, in fact, they disguise it. Why do you think this is?

See if you can find out more about the company Body Map who produced exciting and innovative clothes for young people in the early 1980s.

# The Ethnic Influence in the 1980s

Another important fashion influence during the 1980s was that derived from various ethnic groups and traditional national costumes. Many of the shapes, patterns and colour mixes that occurred during the decade were based on the traditional designs of other countries which had given inspiration to designers for their collections. For example, influence from India inspired collections of sarong skirts, coolie trousers and muslin skirts and tops. There was also a recurrent feeling for peasant clothes which stemmed from regions like Mongolia, Tibet and South America and inspired cold weather clothes in layers of mixed patterns and textures. Ethnic knitwear was also a constant influence with chunky sweaters with a Nordic theme or Fair Isle patterns from Scotland. Other popular items included chunky African jewellery, leather bags from Morocco and silver from the Middle East. On these pages you can see Alma and Adrienne (far right) with two of their friends modelling outfits inspired by the traditional clothes of other countries. Can you think of any more examples like this?

the Latin-American look
with a black-lace mantilla

oriental influence inspires
rich embroidery and texture
as on this evening jacket

peasant clothes inspired
by the Russian tradition

Spanish and prairie tradition –
linen bolero jacket and
trousers, matador straw hat
Navajo blanket

# Pattern and Texture, c. 1985

Here is Adrienne, who now lives in the country permanently, where she has her own business designing and making knitwear and jewellery. She gets most of the inspiration for her work by studying traditional designs from other countries or from the textures and patterns created by nature. She has also been influenced by Kaffe Fassett, a famous knitwear designer, and on the far right you can see her in a style based on one of his designs.

In this picture Adrienne is wearing a woven hat, a thick knitted jumper in cream and brown, a brown corduroy skirt, a leather and silver belt and leather gloves.

On the opposite page she is wearing another outfit which she created herself. Also shown are a leather and silver belt and a silver bracelet which she made.

Adrienne's designs are very colourful and richly patterned. She also likes to experiment with different textures, sometimes weaving them into the same garment.

cream knitted jumper with
embroidery, leather bag with
silver trimmings, woven
striped poncho, fingerless
gloves, wooden beads

multi-coloured
cardigan

black leather belt
with silver

silver and
turquoise
bracelet

# Campaigners and Demonstrators, c. 1985

During the 1980s there was increased concern over environmental and social issues with many people campaigning against such things as drug abuse, nuclear weapons, the technological threat to the environment and famine in third world countries. There were numerous charity events in aid of worthy causes which were promoted and attended by the famous.

These issues had an interesting effect on fashion in that protesters and campaigners, by their over-stated lack of concern for neatness and fashion, seemed to be stating that appearance and grooming were unimportant when it came to saving the world. A good example of this was Bob Geldof, who presented a scruffy and unkempt look for his Live Aid work and created an 'anti-style' image that thousands imitated. Another example was the designer Katherine Hamnett who demonstrated her personal commitment to certain causes with her slogan T-shirts which subsequently became very popular.

Adrienne's cottage is not far from the US airbase at Greenham Common and she often sees some of the women who have been demonstrating against the presence of nuclear weapons. The three protesters shown here present an active image, caring little for fashion or glamour and only about their cause. The two girls on the outside are wearing warm jumpers, anoraks, jeans and leg warmers while the girl in the centre has on a striped wool jumper over tracksuit bottoms and a scarf around her neck. The Greenpeace movement was important in the 1980s. Can you think of any way in which it affected fashion?

# A Yuppie, c. 1987

'Yuppie' was a term used in the 1980s to denote a young, upwardly mobile professional person who would probably be metropolitan, career-minded, ambitious and energetic. Here is Gabrielle whom you last saw on page 27 and who could now be described as a Yuppie. She now has her own hairdressing and beauty salon in London's West End and has a fast moving lifestyle where appearances matter. Clothes are an essential priority for her and she has a vast wardrobe of outfits to suit all her different activities.

In this picture Gabrielle is dressed for work and is wearing a loose-fitting wool jacket with square shoulders, a printed silk blouse, leather skirt and gloves and chunky silver earrings. Gabrielle often wears tailored suits to work which have squared shoulders and slim skirts. This look is very popular and has been described as 'power dressing' as it is appropriate for a competitive career woman.

Gabrielle has a hectic social life and owns many party outfits, one of which you can see pictured opposite. Often she fits in an exercise class or goes running after work, so her wardrobe also contains several sports outfits. She is very conscious of health and skincare and spends freely on make-up and beauty products.

earrings and
bracelet

backless evening dress
with satin bow trim

fitted wool suit,
leather gloves,
silver jewellery

jogging
suit

leather
shoes

# A City Analyst, c. 1987

Here is Geoff, Gabrielle's husband who works in the city as a financial analyst. Geoff earns and spends a great deal of money. Like Gabrielle he is interested in his appearance and owns a vast wardrobe with outfits for all his different activities. In this picture he is dressed for the city and is wearing one of his many suits. This one is double breasted and is made of wool. He also has on a plain cotton shirt and a patterned tie. Gabrielle has given his hair a fashionable look by dyeing the top section blonde and leaving the back and sides naturally dark.

On the opposite page you can see other items from his wardrobe. The chinos that he is wearing on the left are loose fitting and are very popular for casual wear. Originally chinos were woven in Manchester and exported to China, but the Chinese sold supplies back to the Americans stationed in the Philippines just before World War II – hence the name.

striped loose-fitting
shirt, chinos in
heavyweight cotton

wool jacket with
fake fur collar,
wool waistcoat

moleskin trousers

Pierre Cardin shoe
in fine kid leather

casual shoe – in
kid leather

# Sports Clothes, c. 1987

The health and fitness boom that originated in the 1970s continued throughout the 1980s and created a demand for colourful, practical sports clothes which manufacturers were quick to provide. Geoff and Gabrielle enjoy several sporting activities and here they are pictured in some of their sports clothes.

On the right Gabrielle is wearing a cycling suit consisting of a crop top and long shorts in black, pink and lime green. It is made from nylon elastane and therefore fits closely to her body.

Geoff is a keen windsurfer and on the opposite page you can see him in his wet suit. It keeps him warm and dry as it is made from neoprene, a synthetic rubber which is resistant to oil and ageing and is waterproof. The suit also has matching boots and a balaclava.

At the weekends Geoff and Gabrielle go running together in outfits like those shown opposite.

Throughout history sportswear has often become fashion wear and this happened quite frequently during the 1980s. For example, colourful tracksuits and sweatshirts were seen on the streets as well as on the sportsfield, and cycling shorts became fashionable for leisure wear along with head bands, trackshoes and brightly coloured vests.

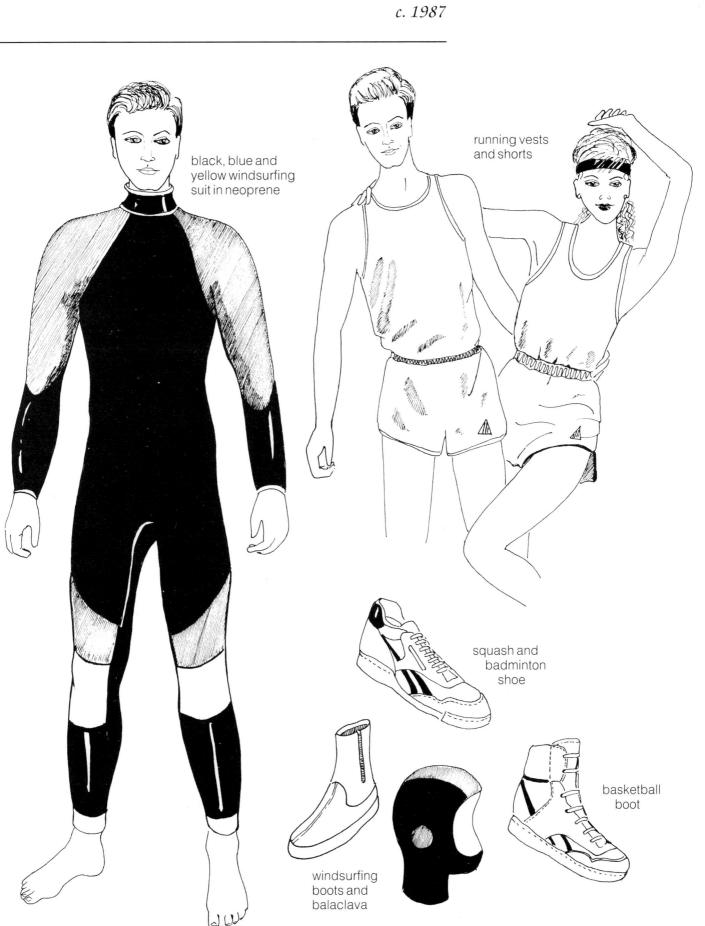

black, blue and yellow windsurfing suit in neoprene

running vests and shorts

squash and badminton shoe

windsurfing boots and balaclava

basketball boot

# Body Dressing, c. 1987

The popularity of aerobics and dance classes also had an important effect on fashion during the 1980s. Leotards and tights of all colours, headbands, wristbands, elasticated belts, jazz shoes, trainers and ballet pumps were worn by the fitness fanatics who created fashion shows in every exercise class.

Many young people liked the feel of these 'second skin' clothes and took to wearing them outside their classes, flaunting their well-exercised figures in closely fitting stretch clothes.

This is Anita, a friend of Gabrielle's who attends several aerobics classes a week. Health and fitness is her way of life and it is reflected in her wardrobe. Here she is wearing a cropped cotton T-shirt with wide sleeves and a pair of knitted leggings. Her hair is loosely held up with a clip, and she has a chunky silver bracelet on her wrist.

On the opposite page you can see her in an outfit that is reminiscent of the 'principal boy' look in ballet or pantomime. It consists of a velvet doublet, tight-fitting stretch trousers and flat black leather shoes. Her wardrobe contains several cross-over tops, boleros and leather pumps, also reminiscent of the 'ballet' look. A new style of bra emerged during the 1980s. It was designed for exercise wear but became fashionable for day wear. It was called a crop top, and one is pictured opposite.

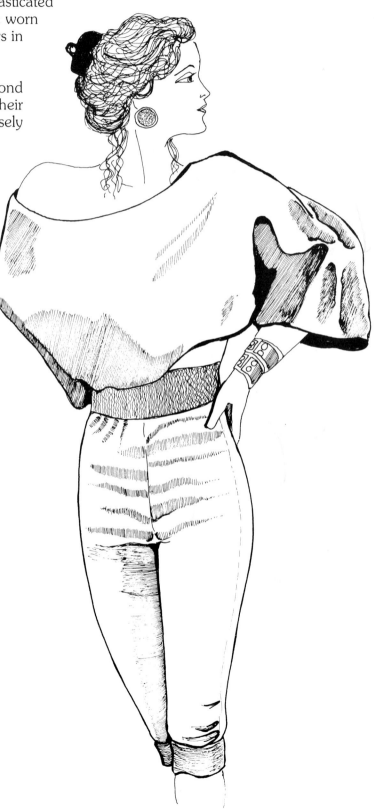

velvet doublet and
tight fitting
stretch trousers

cross-over cotton tops

cotton crop top
and matching
briefs

leather
pumps

# The Return of the Mini, c. 1988

Twenty years after the mini first caught the imagination of a generation of young people in the 1960s it was once again big news in the fashion world. This time however, it was adopted by not only the young but also those old enough to have nostalgic memories of its first life. Magazines sported pictures of Mary Quant, Pauline Stone, Lulu, Cathy McGowan and Una Stubbs, former mini devotees who had again adopted short hemlines, proving that in the 1980s it was not only the young that had the courage and figures to wear them.

The 1980s mini was straighter and more clinging than the 'A' line version of the 1960s and was often worn teamed with men's jackets or thick ribbed tights and heavy flat shoes.

Here is Alma whom you last saw on page 34. She is a model and loves to wear the new mini skirts. In this picture she is wearing a cotton/lycra knit V-back top, a rayon-knit mini, thick tights and leather gloves and shoes. On the opposite page she is pictured with one of her friends who also enjoys the new shorter style skirts.

the 1960s mini

wool suit by
Vivienne Westwood

red and black wool
suit, black cashmere
sweater, silver
bracelet and brooch

# Men's Fashions, c. 1988

This is Alma's boyfriend Richard, who is a male model. He particularly enjoys wearing the current style in casual clothes which are very colourful and comfortable.

In this picture he is wearing a brightly coloured sweater, a cotton shirt and Levi jeans. Denim jeans remained popular with both sexes throughout the 1980s and came in various different styles. For example, it was possible to buy Western style, straight legged or loose fitting jeans depending on your preference.

On the opposite page you can see Richard in two more outfits. On the left he is wearing a waterproof mac, a checked sports coat, a cotton sports shirt and chinos with turn ups. (You might be interested to compare this outfit with that shown on page 54.) On the far right he is wearing a checked Western style shirt, a denim jacket and cotton drill trousers. In hot weather he also enjoys wearing Bermuda shorts which have become very popular.

Many men became more concerned with skincare during the 1980s and cosmetic companies produced ranges of skincare products designed especially for men. Richard sometimes has a cleansing facial with a beauty therapist and regularly uses facial cream. He also occasionally wears make-up when being photographed for the fashion magazines.

52

waterproof coat, sports jacket, chinos

denim jacket with corduroy trim on inner collar and cuffs

Bermuda shorts with elasticated waist

# Girls will be boys . . . c. 1988

Trousers were an interesting feature of women's wardrobes during the 1980s. They came in an assortment of styles and a variety of materials and were adopted by many women for both smart and casual wear.

Here is Kate whom you last saw on page 35. She is quite a tomboy and likes the ease and freedom of trousers. She works in an art gallery and museum and finds that trousers are both practical and warm at work.

In this picture she is wearing a loose trench coat over a checked wool jacket, a linen shirt and cotton chinos. Her hair is cut very short and she prefers to wear only minimal make-up.

Kate is seldom seen in skirts but she does sometimes wear khaki drill shorts teamed with a lace blouse in the summer. If she is going out for the evening she might wear a black velvet trouser suit with a satin shirt. She also might experiment with hair dyes to achieve a more dramatic look.

Other items from her wardrobe are pictured opposite.

collarless shirt
and braces

hair dyed darker
underneath, gold
earrings

double-breasted
trouser suit with
baggy trousers

wool poncho,
polo neck sweater,
trousers

khaki shorts

# Fifties Revival, c. 1988

The 1980s saw the revival of many fashions from previous decades, for example, thirties knitwear, forties-style fitted suits, and the mini from the sixties. There was also a 'fifties revival' with both fashion and music from that era becoming popular with the young.

Here are Kate and her friends wearing some of the latest fifties-style clothes. Kate (this page), is wearing a striped T-shirt with three-quarter length sleeves, jersey trousers which end just below the knee and flat ballet pumps. She has dyed her short hair black, and her gamine appearance is reminiscent of the Audrey Hepburn look of the 1950s.

On the right you can see her friend Samantha in a party outfit and another friend, Jane, in casual clothes. Fifties hairstyles are also popular, with girls wearing the bouffant style or a simple pony tail and boys sporting Elvis quiffs.

It is often easier for designers to escape into a nostalgic past than to look to the future when the present seems uninspiring. There were many fashion revivals in the 1980s – how do you think this reflected society?

56

low-neck stretch top,
black and white
stretch trousers,
canvas shoes with
rope soles

bouffant hairstyle,
stretch top with
cap sleeves,
flared skirt

'50s hairstyles

# Young Fashion, c. 1989

During the late 1980s there was great diversity of fashion amongst the young. They often formed into groups which had different names and were defined as much by their musical taste as by their clothes. Siouxsie and the Banshees, for example, started the 'Gothic' fashion in the early 1980s, but the harsh style, derived from Punk, was adapted and often watered down during the rest of the decade as young people added variations to the original themes.

This is Amy, Gabrielle's sister, who is in the sixth form at school. She is a 'Gothic' or 'Goth' and follows the music of groups like Sisters of Mercy and The Cure. Amy and her friends wear mostly black clothes which often feature tears, fringes and lace and are ornamented with crucifixes. They are keen on suède and can often be seen in fringed suède jackets and suède shoes. They use white make-up on their faces and very black make-up on their eyes and wear onyx or silver jewellery.

In this picture Amy is wearing a black top with lace sleeves over a fringed black T-shirt, a short black jersey mini and torn jersey leggings. She also has on heavy leather boots, but has kept her hair natural. Her friend Lucy (opposite) is wearing a purple mac over a black tunic and mini dress. She has edged the dress and cuffs of her mac with black lace. She also has on thick black tights and suède boots with silver buckles.

Other groups included the 'Trendies' who like to mix and match old and new, wearing second-hand jeans and plain T-shirts with expensive sunglasses and leather jackets.

a 'Trendy'
cropped jacket,
fitted top, baggy,
second-hand jeans

mac with lace on
cuffs, long tunic
over mini dress
edged with lace,
black tights, suède
boots

torn jeans,
patched on
inside

# Conclusion

Towards the end of the 1980s there was a great deal of concern over environmental issues. People began to worry about the many technological advances that had meant the increasing destruction of the world's environment, and there were campaigns to pressurise governments into taking action to 'save the planet'. There were moves towards vegetarianism, organically grown food, clothes made from natural fibres, recycling waste and lead free petrol, and the Green party attracted many more votes from the electorate.

Here is Adrienne with her husband John and their young son Harry. They live in Adrienne's cottage in the country where they grow their own vegetables and keep a few animals. They are wearing loose, comfortable clothes in natural fibres. Adrienne is wearing a hooded tunic top and denim skirt, John has on a cotton tunic, light baggy cotton trousers, a crystal necklace and a waist purse. Little Harry is wearing an identical outfit to his father only in different colours. You might like to compare these clothes to those worn by Adrienne's cousin Gabrielle and her husband (pages 42-45).

Fashion always reflects the spirit of the age like a barometer, and it is interesting therefore that during the 1980s there was no one real 'fashion' that stood out as being representative of the decade. Instead there were numerous different styles that co-existed and many traditional fashion 'rules' were broken. As we have seen, the boundaries between sport and fashion wear dissolved, and traditional athletic shapes appeared in fashion collections. There were 'anti-fashion' inspirations from street style, there was nostalgia for the past with the revival of clothes from previous decades, there was the power dressing of the yuppies contrasted with the unkempt image of campaigners and demonstrators, there were trends set by pop stars and the royal family and even a move towards cross-dressing with the loosening of sexual stereotypes.

With all these different images co-existing, it is worth asking the question: what *is* fashion, and can it survive in this kind of free-for-all? Do women want an imposed look or are they happy to put together odd clothes as they wish?

By the end of the 1980s fashion had become synonymous with style and having the confidence to create and wear an individual look. This is an indication of how much society has changed since the beginning of the century when women were slaves to the dictates of couture.

# Glossary

| | |
|---|---|
| **Barbour** | a waxed cotton jacket, originally designed by John Barbour in 1890, now popular for country wear *(page 21)* |
| **blouson jacket** | a short jacket or top having the shape of a blouse *(page 11)* |
| **brogues** | sturdy shoes, often with ornamental perforations *(pages 9, 22)* |
| **Burberry** | trade name for a light, good quality raincoat *(page 9)* |
| **chinos** | casual baggy cotton trousers *(pages 45, 52, 54)* |
| **crop top** | woman's tight-fitting top ending at the midriff and worn instead of a bra *(pages 46, 49)* |
| **dreadlocks** | hair worn in the Rastafarian style of long matted or tightly curled strands *(page 32)* |
| **D-rings** | rings used to clip on military equipment *(page 9)* |
| **doublet** | a man's close-fitting jacket *(page 49)* |
| **epaulettes** | pieces of ornamental material on the shoulders of a garment *(pages 9, 54)* |
| **gilet** | a waist or hip-length garment, usually sleeveless, fastening up at the front, sometimes made from quilted fabric and designed to be worn over a blouse or shirt *(page 27)* |
| **gothic** | a style of dress adopted by some young people in the late 1980s and featuring black clothes with tears, tatters and fringes *(pages 58, 59)* |
| **mantilla** | a woman's lace or silk scarf covering the hair or the shoulders *(page 36)* |
| **Navajo** | a member of a North American Indian people. See Navajo blanket *(page 37)* |
| **neoprene** | a synthetic rubber which is resistant to oil and ageing and is used in waterproof clothes such as diving suits *(page 47)* |
| **poncho** | a cloak originating in South America and made of a rectangular or circular piece of cloth with a hole in the middle to put the head through *(page 55)* |
| **quiff** | a prominent tuft of hair brushed up above the forehead *(page 57)* |
| **Rastafarian** | a member of a Jamaican religion that regards Ras Tafari (the former emperor Haile Selassie) as a god *(page 32)* |
| **roughneck** | a worker on the floor of an oil rig *(page 17)* |
| **scrunch drying** | a method of hairstyling where the hair is tangled and crumpled when wet to give a thick, curly look when dry *(page 25)* |
| **slashing** | cutting slits into a garment for decoration *(page 14)* |
| **sweatshirt** | a casual sports top usually made of cotton, often fleeced, with a round neckline but no collar and long sleeves *(page 13)* |
| **T-shirt** | an informal sports shirt with wide cut short sleeves, a round, boat or V-neck and usually made in cotton *(pages 13, 32, 40, 48, 56, 58)* |
| **trench coat** | a belted double-breasted waterproof coat resembling a military officer's coat *(pages 9, 54)* |
| **yuppie** | a term used to describe a young, upwardly mobile professional person *(pages 42, 43)* |

# Book List

Barnard, Stephen — *Rock, an illustrated history*, Orbis, 1986
Barwick, Sandra — *A century of style*, George Allen Unwin, 1984
Byrde, Penelope — *A visual history of costume – the twentieth century*, Batsford, 1986
De Marly, Diana — *Fashion for men, an illustrated history*, Batsford, 1985
De La Haye, Amy — *Fashion source book*, MacDonald Orbis, 1988
Dietrich, Jo — *Boy George and Culture Club*, Proteus Books, 1984
Ewing, Elizabeth — *History of 20th century fashion*, Batsford, 1986
Fassett, Kaffe — *Glorious knitting*, Century Publishing, 1985
Greenberg, Keith — *Madonna*, Lerner Publications, 1986
Hillmore, Peter — *Live Aid*, Sidgwick and Jackson, 1985
Hogg, Kate — *Even more dash than cash*, Vogue, 1989
Ireland, Patrick — *Fashion drawing*, 2nd edn., Cambridge University Press, 1984
James, Paul — *Diana: one of the family?*, Sidgwick & Jackson, 1985
Kamin, Philip — *Madonna*, Robus Books, 1985
Keers, Paul — *A gentleman's wardrobe*, Weidenfeld & Nicolson, 1987
McDowell, Colin — *A hundred years of royal style*, Muller, Blond & White, 1985
McDowell, Colin — *McDowell directory of 20th century fashion*, Frederick Muller, 1986
Ribiero, Aileen — *Dress & Morality*, Batsford, 1986
Seddon, Sue (Ed.) — *The complete man*, Ward Lock, 1987
Sunday Times — *Fashion supplement*, March 1988, September 1988, March 1989
Victoria & Albert Museum — *Four hundred years of fashion*, 1984

# Places to Visit

Here are some ideas for interesting places to visit which will help you with your study of dress in the 1980s.

Bath Museum of Costume, Assembly Rooms, Bath, Avon

Gallery of English Costume, Platt Hall, Platt Fields, Rusholme, Manchester M14 5LL

Madame Tussauds, Marylebone Road, London NW1

Museum of London, London Wall, London EC2Y 5HN

Victoria and Albert Museum, Cromwell Road, South Kensington, London SW7 2RL

Also visit your local museum and find out if they have any items of clothing from this period that you could look at.

# Things to Do

1. Find some pictures of the Punk styles of the late 1970s and early 1980s. What features of these styles eventually became fashionable?
2. Look at the knitwear designs on pages 38 and 39. Design a jumper or sweater that is rich in pattern and texture.
3. Find out all you can about these famous designers of the 1980s:
   David and Elizabeth Emanuel, Katherine Hamnett, Rei Kawakubo, Christian Lacroix, Vivienne Westwood, Rifat Ozbek, Jean-Paul Gaultier.
4. Look at the clothes worn by some famous pop stars of the 1980s. How did they influence fashion?
5. Find out more about the ethnic influence on fashion in the 1980s.
6. Find out more about 'street style'. See if you can find any innovative fashion ideas on the streets of your town.
7. How did the Greenpeace and Animal Rights movements affect the clothes people wore in the 1980s?
8. Look at the influence of television, especially soap operas, on fashion in the 1980s.

c. 1980